Snakes and Ladders

Who is winning?

I'm last! Who am I?

100	99	98	97	96	95	94	93	92	91
81	82	83	84	85	86	87	88	89	90
80	79	78	77	76	75	74	73	72	71
61	62	63	64	65	66	67	68	69	70
60	59	58	57	56	55	54	53	52	51
41	42	43	44	45	46	47	48	49	50
40	39	38	37	36	35	34	33	32	31
21	22	23	24	25	26	27	28	29	30
20	19	18	17	16	15	14	13	12	11
1	2	3	4	5	6	7	8	9	10

Jane is on 56.
She throws a 6.
Where does she land?

$56 + 6 = \boxed{62}$

She lands on ☐

Linzi is on 84.
She throws a 4.
Where does she land?

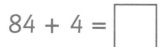

$84 + 4 = $ ☐

She lands on ☐

Marcus is on 72.
He throws a 5.
Where does he land?

$72 + 5 = $ ☐

He lands on ☐

Janus is on 89.
He throws a 3.
Where does he land?

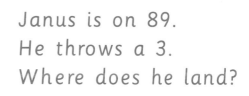

$89 + 3 = $ ☐

He lands on ☐

3

Christmas

There are 42 twinkling lights on the tree and 39 twinkling lights on the wall. How many lights are there altogether?

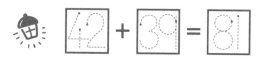 $42 + 39 = 81$

There are ☐ lights.

There are 34 presents under the tree and 29 presents in the sack. How many presents are there altogether?

☐ + ☐ = ☐

There are ☐ presents.

There are 50 cards on the wall and 24 cards on the shelves. How many cards are there altogether?

 ☐ + ☐ = ☐

There are ☐ cards.

There are 30 stars on the tree and 26 stars hanging on the wall. How many stars are there altogether?

 ☐ + ☐ = ☐

There are ☐ stars.

Measuring Lines

Which line do you think is **longest**?
Guess how long it is ☐ cm

Use a **ruler** to measure how long the lines are.

Use a ruler!

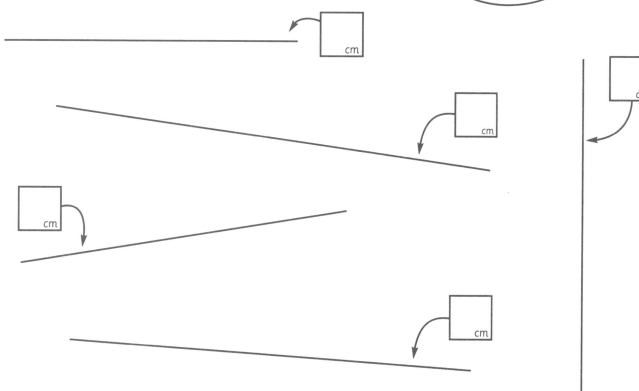

The **longest** line is ☐ cm long.

The **shortest** line is ☐ cm long.

Draw a line 2cm **longer** than the **longest** line.

How long is your ruler?

My line measures ☐ cm long.

5

Pet Shop

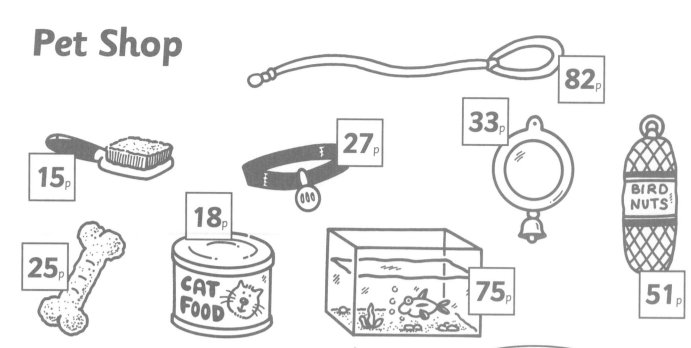

I bought a collar and some food for my cat.
How much did I spend?

$\boxed{27}_p + \boxed{18}_p = \boxed{}_p$

I spent $\boxed{}_p$

I bought a bird's mirror and a brush.

How much did she spend?

$\boxed{}_p + \boxed{}_p = \boxed{}_p$

She spent $\boxed{}_p$

I bought some bird nuts and cat food.

How much did he spend?

$\boxed{}_p + \boxed{}_p = \boxed{}_p$

He spent $\boxed{}_p$

Jenny bought a lead and a brush for her dog.
How much did she spend?

$\boxed{}_p + \boxed{}_p = \boxed{}_p$

Jenny spent $\boxed{}_p$

How much would it cost to buy a bone biscuit and a goldfish?

$\boxed{}_p + \boxed{}_p = \boxed{}_p$

It would cost $\boxed{}_p$ or $\boxed{}_£$

I bought a brush, some bird nuts and a bird's mirror.

How much did he spend?

$\boxed{}_p + \boxed{}_p + \boxed{}_p = \boxed{}_p$

He spent $\boxed{}_p$

The Calendar

May

Sunday	Monday	Tuesday	Wednesday	Thursday	Friday	Saturday
		1	2	3	4	5
6	7	8	9	10	11	12
13	14	15	16	17	18	19
20	21	22	23	24	25	26
27	28	29	30	31		

Write down which day these things happen.

May Day is the first day in May:

_____

Tom's birthday is on the **last** day in May:

_____

The football final is on 5th May:

_____

The garden party is on 20th May:

_____

How many **Tuesdays** in May? ☐

How many **Sundays** in May? ☐

How many days in **May**? ☐

What was the last day in **April**? _____

7

Collectors' Fair

There were 97 bean toys. 29 were sold.

How many were left?

Buy me, I'm cute!

☐7 − 2☐ = ☐

There were ☐ left.

There were 25 cars in boxes and 16 cars not in boxes.

How many cars were there altogether?

☐ + ☐ = ☐

There were ☐ cars altogether.

At the beginning of the day Mark had 87 stamps.

I sold 35 stamps

How many stamps were left?

☐ − ☐ = ☐

There were ☐ left.

MATHS IS FUN!

There were 65 badges on the stall.

36 were sold.

I ♥ BADGES

How many badges were left?

☐ − ☐ = ☐

There were ☐ badges left.

12 gold coins

2 medals

10 silver coins

How many things were sold on this stall?

☐ + ☐ + ☐ = ☐

☐ were sold altogether.

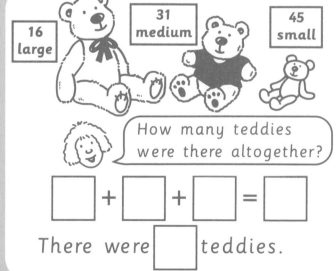

16 large

31 medium

45 small

How many teddies were there altogether?

☐ + ☐ + ☐ = ☐

There were ☐ teddies.

More Measuring

Use a ruler to measure these things.

This worm is [ ] cm long.

Draw a worm 3cm **longer**.

My worm measures [ ] cm long.

This slug is [ ] cm long.

Draw a slug 1cm **shorter**.

My slug measures [ ] cm long.

This centipede is [ ] cm long.

Draw a centipede 3cm longer.

My centipede measures [ ] cm long.

The flagpole is [ ] cm tall.

Draw a flagpole **half** as tall.

My flagpole is [ ] cm tall.

9

Area

Write the **area** of each letter.

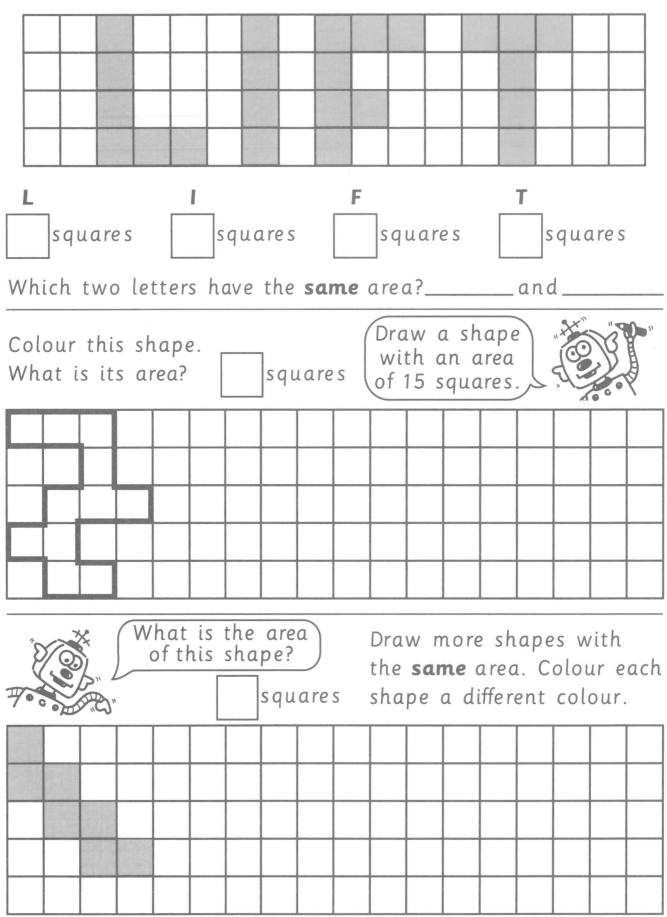

L [ ] squares   I [ ] squares   F [ ] squares   T [ ] squares

Which two letters have the **same** area? _____ and _____

Colour this shape.
What is its area? [ ] squares

Draw a shape
with an area
of 15 squares.

What is the area
of this shape? [ ] squares

Draw more shapes with
the **same** area. Colour each
shape a different colour.

Busy Aliens!

50 space worms   **17 space worms**

How many space worms did she find **altogether**?

$\boxed{50} + \boxed{17} = \boxed{}$ space worms.

She found $\boxed{}$ space worms.

I can see 63 red stars and 28 blue stars.

How many stars **altogether**?

$\boxed{} + \boxed{} = \boxed{}$ stars.

He can see $\boxed{}$ stars.

Last week I saw 19 meteors.   This week I've seen 67 meteors.

How many meteors has Arno seen **altogether**?

$\boxed{} + \boxed{} = \boxed{}$ meteors.

He saw $\boxed{}$ meteors.

There are 25 aliens in each rocket.

What is the **total** number of aliens in all three rockets?

$\boxed{} + \boxed{} + \boxed{} = \boxed{}$ aliens.

There are $\boxed{}$ aliens.

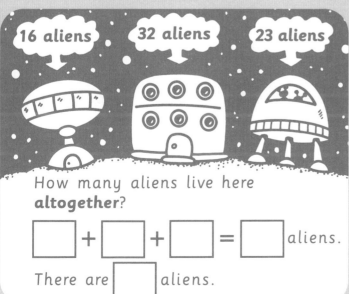

16 aliens   **32 aliens**   **23 aliens**

How many aliens live here **altogether**?

$\boxed{} + \boxed{} + \boxed{} = \boxed{}$ aliens.

There are $\boxed{}$ aliens.

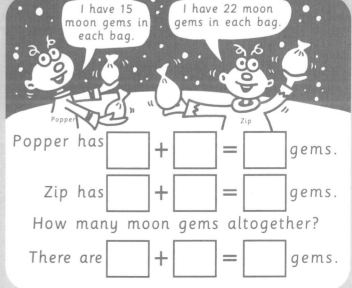

I have 15 moon gems in each bag.   I have 22 moon gems in each bag.

Popper   Zip

Popper has $\boxed{} + \boxed{} = \boxed{}$ gems.

Zip has $\boxed{} + \boxed{} = \boxed{}$ gems.

How many moon gems altogether?

There are $\boxed{} + \boxed{} = \boxed{}$ gems.

The Fairground

Sam and her friends each took £1.00 to the fair. They could have 1 turn each. How much did they take home?

Joel went on the dodgems. How much change did he have?

£1.00 − $\boxed{75}$ p = $\boxed{}$ p

He had $\boxed{}$ p change.

Victoria whizzed down the bouncy slide. How much change did she have?

£1.00 − $\boxed{}$ p = $\boxed{}$ p

She had $\boxed{}$ p change.

Emil was scared on the ghost train. How much change did he have?

£1.00 − $\boxed{}$ p = $\boxed{}$ p

He had $\boxed{}$ p change.

Alice went round on the big wheel. How much change did she have?

£1.00 − $\boxed{}$ p = $\boxed{}$ p

She had $\boxed{}$ p change.

Sam tried her strength and hit the bell. How much change did she have?

£1.00 − $\boxed{}$ p = $\boxed{}$ p

She had $\boxed{}$ p change.

Isabel loved her ride on the merry-go-round. How much change did she have?

£1.00 − $\boxed{}$ p = $\boxed{}$ p

She had $\boxed{}$ p change.

Party Time

Gina and Tim shared a party at the Village Hall. There were 26 boys and 26 girls there. How many children were there? 26 + 26 = ☐ . There were ☐ children.

Tim had 20 cards and Gina had 35 cards. How many cards were there altogether?

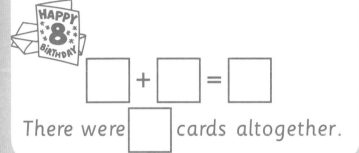

☐ + ☐ = ☐

There were ☐ cards altogether.

The boys ate 2 sausages each and the girls ate 1 sausage each. How many sausages were eaten?

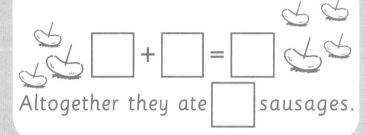

☐ + ☐ = ☐

Altogether they ate ☐ sausages.

There were 55 balloons. The children burst 30. How many were left?

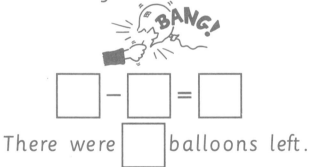

☐ − ☐ = ☐

There were ☐ balloons left.

17 boys wore cowboy hats and 9 boys wore American Indian headdresses. How many more boys wore cowboy hats than headdresses?

☐ − ☐ = ☐

☐ more boys wore cowboy hats.

12 girls wore party dresses and 14 girls wore trousers. How many more girls wore trousers than dresses?

☐ − ☐ = ☐

☐ more girls wore trousers.

36 children joined in the disco. How many children sat and watched?

☐ − ☐ = ☐

☐ children sat and watched.

13

Saving and Spending

I bought an ice cream with a 50p coin.

25p

How much change did I have?

$\boxed{50}_p - \boxed{25}_p = \boxed{}_p$

I had $\boxed{}_p$ change.

I had £1.00. I spent 68p.

How much did I have left?

$\boxed{}_£ - \boxed{}_p = \boxed{}_p$

I had $\boxed{}_p$ left.

Anwar earned £1.00 by weeding.

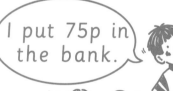
I put 75p in the bank.

How much did he have left to spend?

$\boxed{}_£ - \boxed{}_p = \boxed{}_p$

He had $\boxed{}_p$ left to spend.

I saved 10p a week for six weeks.

How much did I save?

$\boxed{}_p \times \boxed{} = \boxed{}_p$

I saved $\boxed{}_p$

I collected money for Guide Dogs.

Mum 20p
Luke 25p
Fran 50p
Amy 5p

How much did I collect **altogether**?

$\boxed{}_p$
$\boxed{}_p$
$\boxed{}_p$
$\boxed{}_p$
$\overline{\boxed{}_p}$

I collected $\boxed{}_p$

Lucy had a pound coin. She bought two pencils.

10p

How much did she have left?

$\boxed{}_£ - \boxed{}_p = \boxed{}_p$

She had $\boxed{}_p$ left.

How Old?

How many years do Mum's and Dad's ages add up to?

$$\boxed{38} + \boxed{42} = \boxed{}$$

They add up to $\boxed{}$ years.

How old was Mum when Barney was born?

$$\boxed{} - \boxed{} = \boxed{}$$

She was $\boxed{}$ years old.

How much **older** is Dad than Mum?

$$\boxed{} - \boxed{} = \boxed{}$$

Dad is $\boxed{}$ years **older** than Mum.

Gran is 9 years **younger** than Grandpa.
How old is Grandpa?

$$\boxed{} + \boxed{} = \boxed{}$$

Grandpa is $\boxed{}$ years old.

15

Measuring Liquids

How many millilitres (ml) of juice are in the jug? ☐ ml

How many more millilitres would you need to fill the jug? ☐ ml

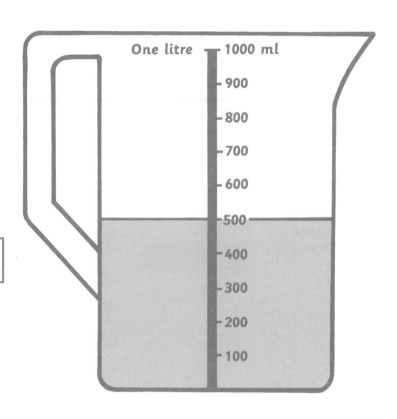

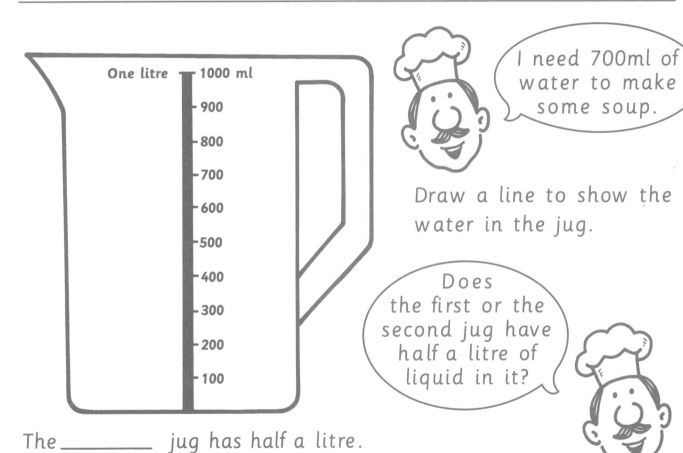

I need 700ml of water to make some soup.

Draw a line to show the water in the jug.

Does the first or the second jug have half a litre of liquid in it?

The _____ jug has half a litre.

Multi-Storey Car Park

Each level has a different number of spaces.

Level 4	18 spaces
Level 3	21 spaces
Level 2	39 spaces
Level 1	22 spaces

CAR PARK

How many cars can Levels 1 and 2 hold?

$$39 + 22 = \boxed{}$$

Levels 1 and 2 hold $\boxed{}$ cars.

How many cars can Levels 3 and 4 hold?

$$\boxed{} + \boxed{} = \boxed{}$$

Levels 3 and 4 hold $\boxed{}$ cars.

How many cars can the car park hold **altogether**? $\boxed{} + \boxed{} + \boxed{} + \boxed{} = \boxed{}$

The car park can hold $\boxed{}$ cars.

At 4 o'clock Level 3 was **full** then 5 cars leave.
How many cars are left on Level 3?

$$\boxed{} - \boxed{} = \boxed{}$$

There are $\boxed{}$ left on Level 3.

There are only 15 cars still in the car park at 7 o'clock.
How many spaces are empty?

$$\boxed{} - \boxed{} = \boxed{}$$

There are $\boxed{}$ spaces empty.

| CAR PARK SPACES | |
Level	Empty Spaces
1	4
2	10
3	2
4	15

How many empty spaces are there on this list?

$$\boxed{} + \boxed{} + \boxed{} + \boxed{} = \boxed{}$$

How many cars are still there? $\boxed{} - \boxed{} = \boxed{}$

Weighing

How **heavy** is Jim's sack?

☐ g + ☐ g = ☐ kg

How much will the contents of the basket weigh when the packet of tea is added?

☐ g + ☐ g + ☐ g = ☐ g

What is the weight of the third package if all three packages together weigh 1kg?

☐ g + ☐ g = ☐ g

☐ kg − ☐ g = ☐ g

The third package weighs ☐ g

Car Boot Sale

Books 5p each

Lamp 20p
Hammer 21p

Bag 45p
Mug 14p

CDs 20p each
Plates 8p each

Dartboard 30p
Teapot 25p
Ball 9p

Magazines 2p each

Rachel bought 3 things for her mum. She spent 90p. What did she buy?

She bought _____ 20p

_____ 25p

+ 45p

□ p

How much did Mum spend?

Mum bought 2 plates □ p

a hammer □ p

a mug □ p

a ball □ p

2 CDs + □ p

She spent □ £   □ £

Zoe had 50p.
She bought the dartboard □ p
and 2 books □ p

□ p + □ p = □ p

How much change did she have? □ p

William bought 10 magazines and 4 books.

Magazines cost □ p × □ = □ p

Books cost □ p × □ = □ p

How much did he spend?

□ p + □ p = □ p

He spent □ p

19

Right Angles

I'm a right angle!

Mark all the **right angles** with a red cross **X**.

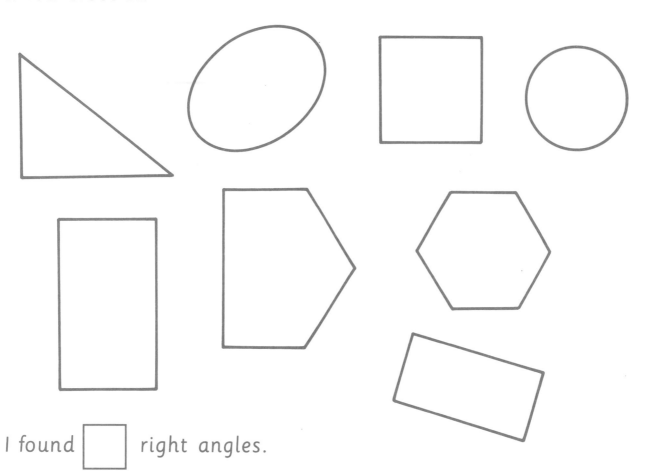

I found ☐ right angles.

Follow Robodog's path. Mark the right-angle turns 'R' in red.

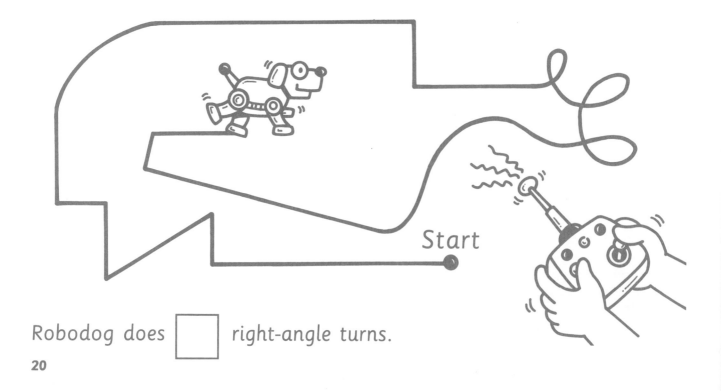

Start

Robodog does ☐ right-angle turns.

20

Just Numbers!

Put the rest of these numbers in the shapes to add up to 100.

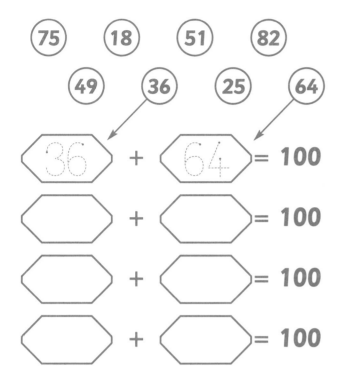

(75) (18) (51) (82)

(49) (36) (25) (64)

⬡ 36 ⬡ + ⬡ 64 ⬡ = **100**

⬡ ⬡ + ⬡ ⬡ = **100**

⬡ ⬡ + ⬡ ⬡ = **100**

⬡ ⬡ + ⬡ ⬡ = **100**

Think of 2 numbers to make each sum correct.

(5) × (2) = **10**

( ) × (2) = **24**

( ) + (2) = **75**

( ) ÷ (2) = **2**

Write these numbers **in order** on the ladder. Start at the bottom with the **smallest**.

702

538

600

585

Going up!

557

642

755

Smallest

Use 4 cards to make a **total less than** 100.

| 3 1 | + | 4 6 | = | | |

Use 4 cards to make a **total more than** 30.

| | | + | | | = | | |

Use 4 cards to make a **total between 40 and 50.**

| | | + | | | = | | |

Activity Time

Jack started at 12 o'clock.
What time did he finish?

_____

Debjani rode for 1 hour.
What time did she finish?

_____

Mark set off at 10 o'clock.
What time did he get home?

_____

Emily went to
ballet at 7 o'clock.
What time did she finish?

_____

The match
began at half past nine.
What time did the match end?

_____

Rocco went
roller-blading for 1½ hours.
What time did he finish?

_____

Bus Fares

Destination	Single	Return
Winton	25p	45p
Zoo	50p	90p
Hadfield	30p	55p
Rookwood	47p	85p
Dogs half price		

I took Alfie to the vet in Hadfield.

Alfie

Mrs Smith bought **single** tickets.
How much did the tickets cost?

Mrs Smith   Alfie   Total

30 p + ☐ p = ☐ p

The tickets cost ☐ p

We each have £1.00.

Can giraffes go for half price too?

They bought return tickets to the Zoo.
How much change did they each have?

☐ £ − ☐ p = ☐ p   They each had ☐ p change.

How much **change** did they have altogether? ☐ p

Georgia bought a **return** ticket to Rookwood.
How much **change** did she have from £1.00?

I have a pound coin.

☐ £ − ☐ p = ☐ p

She had ☐ p change.

John

I went to Winton.

I went to Rookwood.

Harry

Both men bought **single** tickets.
How much more did Harry's ticket cost?

☐ p − ☐ p = ☐ p

It cost ☐ p more.

23

Odd and Even

Write these numbers
in the correct set.

137   51   211   48   329

73   405   94   26   52

Odd numbers

Numbers less
than 100

Look at
these
numbers.

(6)   (13)   (8)   (9)

(7)   (10)   (12)   (11)

Which of these numbers are **even**?

◯ ◯ ◯ ◯

What is the **total** of the **even** numbers?

◯ + ◯ + ◯ + ◯ = ◯

What is the **total** of the **odd** numbers?

◯ + ◯ + ◯ + ◯ = ◯

Lunch Time!

They haven't enough money!

Jake has 15p. He wants to buy a banana. How much **more** money does he need?

$$\boxed{22}\text{p} - \boxed{15}\text{p} = \boxed{}\text{p}$$

He needs $\boxed{}$p more.

Sara has 20p. She wants a hot dog. How much **more** money does she need?

$$\boxed{}\text{p} - \boxed{}\text{p} = \boxed{}\text{p}$$

She needs $\boxed{}$p more.

Gary wants a drink. He has 28p. How much **more** money does he need?

$$\boxed{}\text{p} - \boxed{}\text{p} = \boxed{}\text{p}$$

He needs $\boxed{}$p more.

Cara wants some crisps and a salad. She only has 80p. How much **more** money does she need?

$$\boxed{}\text{p} - \boxed{}\text{p} = \boxed{}\text{p}$$

She needs $\boxed{}$p more.

Nasser has 67p. He wants some pasta and an apple. How much **more** money does he need?

$$\boxed{}\text{p} - \boxed{}\text{p} = \boxed{}\text{p}$$

He needs $\boxed{}$p more.

Lisa has 74p. She wants some chips and a hamburger. How much **more** money does she need?

$$\boxed{}\text{£} - \boxed{}\text{p} = \boxed{}\text{p}$$

She needs $\boxed{}$p more.

Favourite Fruits

The children did a survey to find out which fruit was the favourite in their class.

 6 liked kiwi fruit best.

 4 girls liked peaches best.

 Apples got 10 votes.

9 said bananas. 2 children liked pears most.

Only I liked oranges best.

Finish the **bar chart** to show this data. Use different colours.

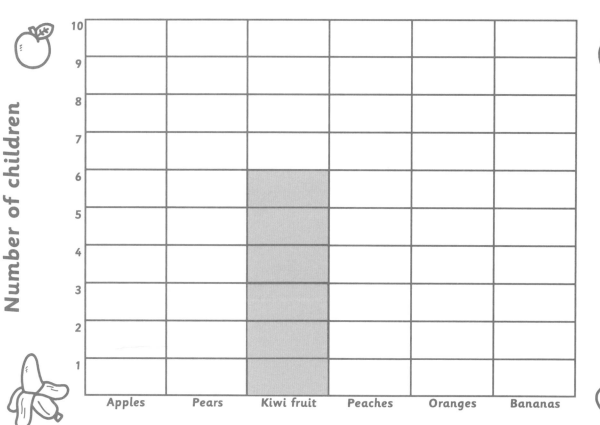

Which was the **most popular** fruit? _____

How many **more** children liked bananas rather than peaches? ☐

How many **more** children chose apples rather than kiwi fruit? ☐

Which fruit in the chart was the **least** favourite? _____

What is your favourite fruit?

Money Boxes

Find out how much money is in each money box.
Then work out how much **more** money is needed to make £1.00.

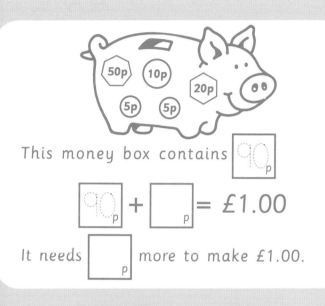

This money box contains [90]p

[90]p + [ ]p = £1.00

It needs [ ]p more to make £1.00.

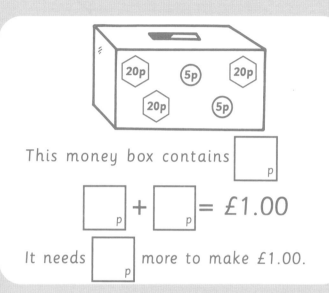

This money box contains [ ]p

[ ]p + [ ]p = £1.00

It needs [ ]p more to make £1.00.

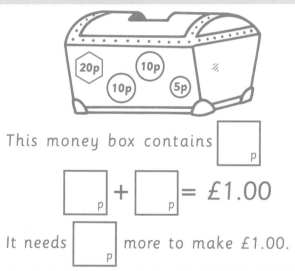

This money box contains [ ]p

[ ]p + [ ]p = £1.00

It needs [ ]p more to make £1.00.

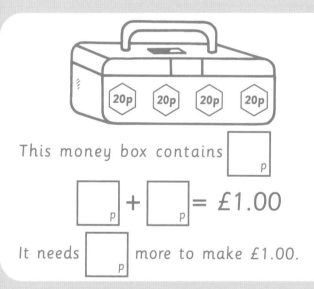

This money box contains [ ]p

[ ]p + [ ]p = £1.00

It needs [ ]p more to make £1.00.

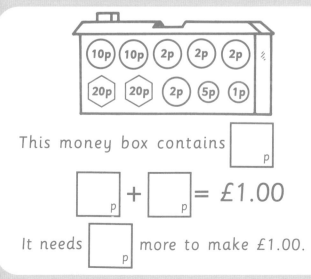

This money box contains [ ]p

[ ]p + [ ]p = £1.00

It needs [ ]p more to make £1.00.

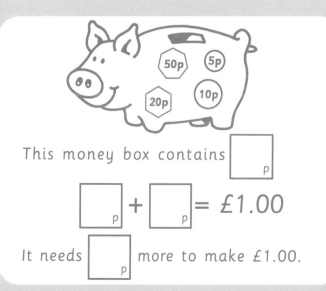

This money box contains [ ]p

[ ]p + [ ]p = £1.00

It needs [ ]p more to make £1.00.

Triangles

Join the three circled dots · to make a **smaller** triangle inside the larger one.

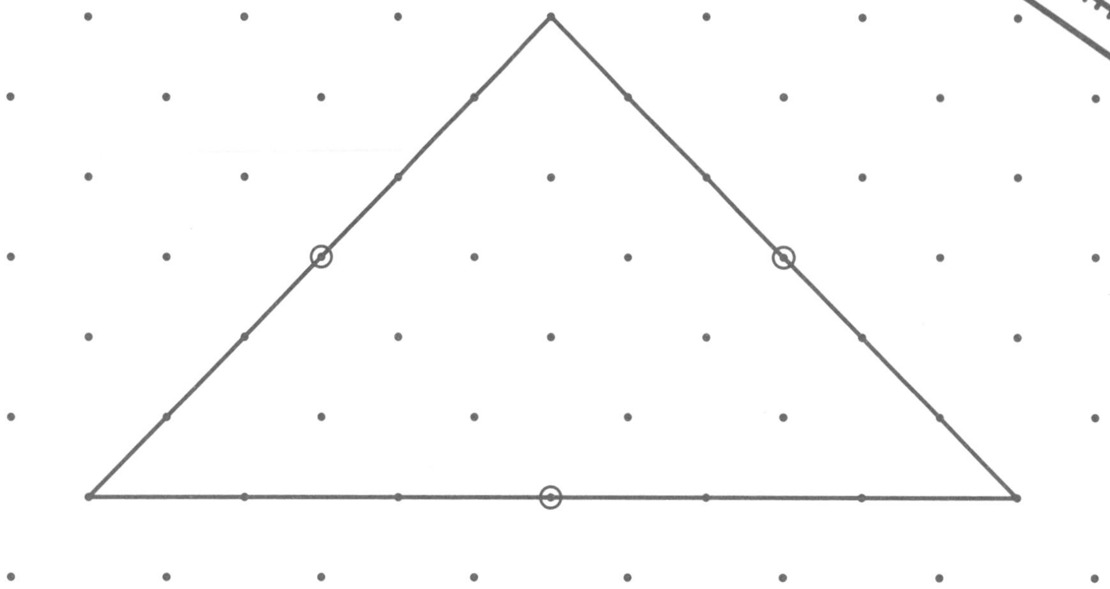

Use a ruler!

How many triangles are there **altogether**? ☐ triangles

Join the crosses in the triangle to make a **smaller** triangle.
Now make a **larger** triangle by joining the circled dots.

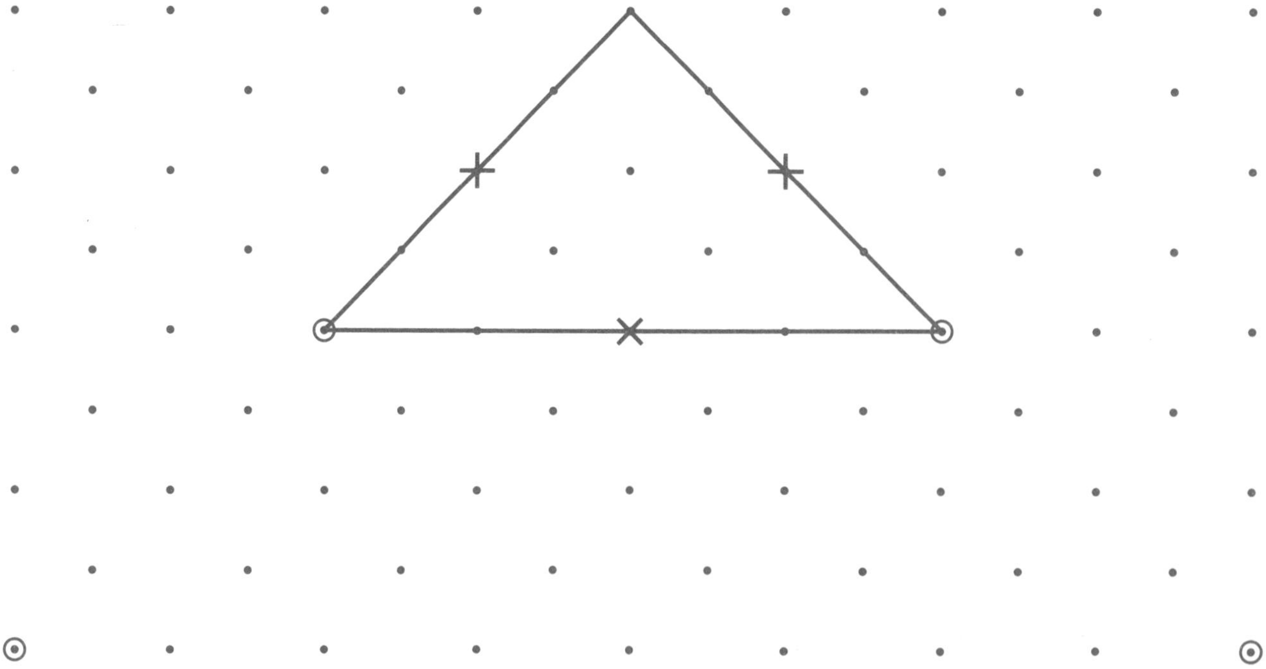

How many triangles are there **altogether**? ☐ triangles

How many **more** triangles can you make? ☐ triangles

28

Visiting Friends

Kate visited Tom and Laura.
How many **miles** did she travel **altogether**?

[40] + [32] = [ ] miles. She travelled [ ] miles.

I'm going to Tom's and Laura's.

Kate

I went to Joe's...

...then on to Kate's

Laura

How many **miles** did Laura travel altogether?

[ ] + [ ] = [ ] miles.

She travelled [ ] miles.

Tom's going to see Kate then Joe.

How many **miles** will Tom travel **altogether**?

[ ] + [ ] = [ ] miles

He will travel [ ] miles.

Joe went to Laura's and back home.
Then he went to Kate's.

How far did I travel?

[ ] + [ ] + [ ] = [ ] miles.

Joe travelled [ ] miles.

Joe

I went to Kate's then went home.

How many **miles** did Tom travel **altogether**?

[ ] + [ ] = [ ] miles. He travelled [ ] miles.

Tom

29

Beach Shop

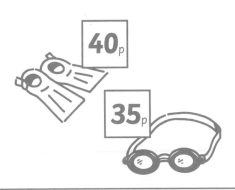     

Liam had £1.00. How many balls could he buy?

$\boxed{20_p} \times \boxed{} = £1.00$ So he could buy $\boxed{}$ balls.

I have 68p. I want to buy as many postcards as I can. How many postcards can I buy?

$\boxed{}_p \times \boxed{} = \boxed{}_p$

I can buy $\boxed{}$ postcards.

I have $\boxed{}_p$ left.

Mia had 60p. She bought some armbands. How much money did she have left?

$\boxed{}_p - \boxed{}_p = \boxed{}_p$

What could she buy with the change? _____

Ben wanted to buy each of his 5 friends a frisbee.

$\boxed{}_p \times \boxed{} = \boxed{}_p$ Ben spent $\boxed{}_p$

 How much did I spend?

 I spent £1.00.

Andy bought 3 different things. What did he buy?

$\boxed{}_p + \boxed{}_p + \boxed{}_p = £1.00$

He bought _____ , _____ and _____ .

Jack's Day

How many hours are there in a day?

☐ hours

This part is one hour

How many hours does Jack spend

at school? ☐   playing the piano? ☐

eating? ☐   doing homework? ☐

What does he spend most time doing? _____

How much more time do I spend playing football than watching TV?   ☐ hours.

How long do **you** spend sleeping?   ☐ hours.

How many hours are you awake?   ☐ hours.

Schofield&Sims

the long-established educational publisher
specialising in maths, English and science materials for schools

Key Stage 1 Problem Solving is a series of graded activity books that helps
children to sharpen their mathematical skills by applying their knowledge to a range
of 'real-life' situations, such as shopping and telling the time.

Key Stage 1 Problem Solving Book 3 includes:

- Addition and subtraction to 100
- Using a hundred square
- Measuring with a ruler
- Counting money, converting pence to pounds and calculating change
- Reading a calendar
- Right angles
- Odd and even numbers.

This book is suitable for children in Key Stage 1.

The full range of titles in the series is as follows:

KS1 Problem Solving Book 1:   ISBN 978 07217 0922 2

KS1 Problem Solving Book 2:   ISBN 978 07217 0923 9

KS1 Problem Solving Book 3:   ISBN 978 07217 0924 6

Have you tried the **Number Books** by Schofield & Sims?
This series helps children to learn basic calculation skills including
addition, subtraction, multiplication and division.

**For further information and to place your order
visit www.schofieldandsims.co.uk or telephone 01484 607080**

ISBN 978-07217-0924-6

9 780721 709246

Schofield&Sims

Dogley Mill, Fenay Bridge, Huddersfield HD8 0NQ
Phone: 01484 607080 Facsimile: 01484 606815
E-mail: sales@schofieldandsims.co.uk
www.schofieldandsims.co.uk

ISBN 978 07217 0924 6

£2.45
(Retail price)

Key Stage 1
Age range: 5–7 years